The Eerie Singing Sirens

Written by John Parsons
Illustrated by James Hart

Contents

For learning solutions, visit **cengage.com.au**

Meet the Characters

Timoneus

A seafarer in Ancient Greece.

Odysseus

A hero from Ancient Greece.

The Three Sirens

Strange and dangerous creatures, half-bird and half-human.

Dear Reader

Odysseus was a famous ancient Greek hero who had many amazing adventures. Often, the stories that are told about him have a lesson or moral.

In this story, I've written about a friend of Odysseus's. See if you can spot the moral of the story, right at the end.

John Parsons

Author

The Adventures of Timoneus

1. Ancient Greek port
2. Mediterranean Sea
3. Jagged rocks
4. Island of Anthemusa

1 Strange Things

This story of Timoneus, a famous ancient seafarer, begins in his young days.

A month after he reached the age of ten years, Timoneus was called to be a young seafarer with one of Greece's most famous heroes: Odysseus.

"In your journeys, you shall know many adventures and discover a wealth of strange things," confided Odysseus to Timoneus. And he was right, as this tale will tell.

For many years, Timoneus learnt his seafarer's craft with Odysseus. One day, a beautiful golden sunrise spread above the Mediterranean horizon.

"Today, we sail to the mysterious and dangerous island of Anthemusa," said Odysseus. "There, I shall listen to the dangerous, haunting songs of the Sirens."

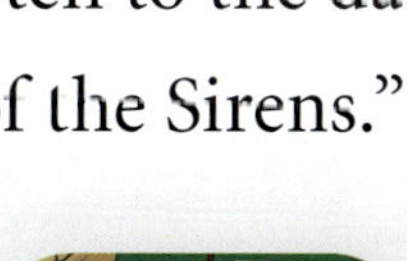

Fear struck Timoneus's heart. The Sirens were half-bird, half-woman. They sang a song so beautiful it lured helpless seafarers onto the jagged rocks and steep cliffs that surrounded Anthemusa.

"It is said that these songs of pleasure end with nothing good!" said Timoneus.

"Fear not!" replied Odysseus. "I have a plan."

Timoneus and the rest of the crew took their seats, and rowed. The sails were hoisted and a breeze blew. They sailed towards the fabled Sirens.

Odysseus took a lump of beeswax and kneaded it until it was soft. Then he told his men to plug their ears with it, and to tie him to the mast of the ship.

"No matter what I do or say, do not stop or untie me," ordered Odysseus.

2 A Haunting Song

Timoneus and the crew did as the wise Odysseus asked. Suddenly, the wind dropped. The sea became calm. None of the men could hear, so Timoneus waved at them to row.

When the ship was within a shout from the island, the Sirens spied Odysseus, Timoneus and the crew. They began to sing.

A beautiful, haunting song filled Odysseus's ears. His heart felt as if it was going to burst with joy.

"Come to us, come to us, oh Odysseus," the Sirens sang. "Come closer and listen to our song. Come closer and hear our sweet voices. Odysseus, Odysseus. Come to our field of flowers and hear the song that we shall sing to you."

Odysseus could not resist the song of the Sirens. He called out to his men to untie him.
Even though he could see the waves smashing upon the jagged rocks of the island, every urge in his body told him to sail towards the Sirens. Their song was so beautiful that nothing else mattered.

But the men could not hear Odysseus. Timoneus and the men ignored his struggles. The ship sailed past the island and out of danger. Odysseus returned to his senses and smiled at Timoneus and his crew.

That evening, they heard all about the enchanting, haunting song – from the lips of the only person that had ever heard the Sirens' song and lived.

3 One Glorious Day

In time, Timoneus became master of his own ship. He visited every port across the shimmering silvery Mediterranean sea.

But he never forgot the sight of Odysseus, his eyes lighting up in delight the moment he heard the Sirens' song.

"If I could bring these Sirens on my journeys and make them sing for the people in the ports I visit, I would become a very rich man," Timoneus said to himself. "Everyone would be drawn to come and hear them. Surely, no harm would come if the Sirens were aboard my ship, instead of luring seafarers towards rocks or cliffs."

And so, one glorious day, when a beautiful golden sunrise rose above the Mediterranean horizon, Timoneus and his crew set sail to the mysterious and dangerous island of Anthemusa.

"Fear not!" said Timoneus to his crew, in an echo of his old master, Odysseus. "I have a plan."

Just like the day thirty years before, the ship's crew took their seats and began to row. The sails were hoisted and a breeze came. And soon, the island of Anthemusa was on the horizon.

Timoneus also carried a lump of beeswax – but, unlike Odysseus, he did not wish to

hear the Sirens until they were captured. He told his men to plug their ears, and he did the same.

Soon the ship was so close to the island that the crew could smell the sweet perfume of the flowers in the meadows. The Sirens spied Timoneus and his crew. They started to sing.

4 Come Closer

But none of the men aboard could hear the Sirens' song. Timoneus called out.

"It is I, Timoneus, who has come back, my Sirens, after many years. Come to me, come to me. I shall take you to places where you shall learn many strange things."

The Sirens fell silent.

"You shall sing in lands all around this great sea. Your sweet melodies shall enthral and enchant crowds. In every port and city, crowds of people will want to listen to your sweet songs."

Still, there was no answer.

"Sirens, you shall be famous forever. Long after the cities of ancient Greece have crumbled and turned to dust, people all over the world shall speak of your song," called Timoneus.

Then, three strange creatures started to wade through the water, out to sea. They had long flowing hair, and wings. Their bodies were half-human and half-bird.

"Come closer," called Timoneus. He waved to his men to ready their ropes and chains, which they had hidden beneath their benches.

The ship drifted closer to the Sirens. Timoneus ordered his men to row towards the creatures, so that the Sirens would not vanish beneath the waves. Finally, the Sirens climbed aboard. Their piercing eyes looked at Timoneus and his crew, and their long, flowing hair blew in the breeze.

“Now!” yelled Timoneus. He dropped his arm in a signal. The crew leapt to their feet and rushed forward. Within the time it took for a single wave to pass, the Sirens were captured and were made to sit on the deck, wailing mournfully.

“The gods are smiling upon me,” thought Timoneus. The Sirens were his! He would become rich as they sang to people in every port.

And when he was satisfied the Sirens could not escape, he took the beeswax from his ears. The crew did the same.

5 Gather Your Souls

That was the wrong thing to do. The Sirens had not lost their slyness or become less dangerous.

As Anthemusa disappeared over the horizon, the Sirens sobbed. A soft, mournful song began to escape their lips. The men stopped rowing.

"Oh wise Timoneus," the Sirens sang. "Our voices and our songs belong to you. We shall sing our sweet songs for you. But, Timoneus, Timoneus, you must let us return one more time to our field of flowers. There, we shall gather our souls – for they remain in Anthemusa and it is our souls that fill our songs with enchantment."

Timoneus could not resist the pleading of the Sirens. He told his men to turn around.

"I shall keep this Siren, Ligeia, aboard my ship while you return," he said to the other Sirens. "Gather your souls and return to me."

Thinking he was safe, Timoneus allowed the other Sirens to slip into the water.

But when they did, the wind dropped and the sea became calm.

Suddenly, a beautiful, haunting song filled Timoneus's ears. His heart felt as if it would burst with joy.

"Come with us, come with us, oh Timoneus," the Sirens sang. "Come to our island. Listen to our song. Come with us, come to our field of flowers. Hear the song that we will sing to you."

And it dawned upon Timoneus at that moment, that the story of the most famous of all the ancient seafarers would soon end.

Timoneus tried to find his beeswax again, to no avail. He could not resist the song of the Sirens, who had so cleverly escaped him. Even though he could see the dangerous waves smashing upon the jagged rocks of the island, every urge in his body told him to follow the Sirens, as they swam back to shore. Their song was so beautiful that nothing else mattered.

As the haunting song filled every space in his body, a memory entered his head.

"In your journeys, you shall know many strange things," Odysseus had once said to him. And he was right, as this adventure showed.

Ligeia, the Siren he had kept on board, smiled at him.

“Now you and your crew will follow *our* singing and be *our* captives,” she said.

To this day, the Sirens remain known all around the world. The cities of ancient Greece have long since crumbled, turned to dust and disappeared. Yet people still speak of their beautiful songs – and now you know the tale and will keep it alive.

But beware! Learn from Odysseus's wisdom and Timoneus's foolishness. The results of giving in to temptation can last much longer than the fleeting pleasure of the temptation itself!

THE END